AF211891

JUDE LARRIE

COACHING BUSINESS

The Ultimate Guide on How to Run a Successful Coaching Business, Learn the Best Practices and Effective Methods to Sell Your Coaching Services

Descrierea CIP a Bibliotecii Naționale a României
JUDE LARRIE
   COACHING BUSINESS. The Ultimate Guide on How to Run a Successful Coaching Business, Learn the Best Practices and Effective Methods to Sell Your Coaching Services / Jude Larrie – Bucharest: Editura My Ebook, 2021
   ISBN

JUDE LARRIE

COACHING BUSINESS

The Ultimate Guide on How to Run a Successful Coaching Business, Learn the Best Practices and Effective Methods to Sell Your Coaching Services

My Ebook Publishing House
Bucharest, 2021

TABLE OF CONTENTS

INTRODUCTION

When you've enjoyed and become successful in a specific line of work and think you could make a positive impact teaching others to do the same thing, you may want to think about branching out to make coaching a part of your business plan. If coaching is an option you'd like to try, this guide, Running a Coaching Business: An Introductory Guide to Running Your First Coaching Program" is a must to read.

The guide is an introduction to the lucrative and satisfying world of online coaching if you want to become a coach of Internet marketers, life coaching or business coaching.

You'll learn that it takes more than a desire to help people to become a success at online coaching - and discover the strategies that will help propel you to coaching success.

There are some people who are just meant to be coaches. You've likely experienced the sports coach, math coach or life coach who has a way of explaining things so that light bulbs are continuously lighting up in your brain.

For some coaches, it's the style that makes them stand out and for others it might be the magic rapport between the coach and his or her students when the teacher is presenting information in a way that stimulates and challenges the mind.

Coaches who are already established in a thriving business can also learn from this guide because there are new trends and tips about the marketing and business end that can benefit even more experienced coaches.

If you're already an online entrepreneur, creating a coaching program as a branch of your business can be a great way to increase your online visibility, standing in the online community and also to increase revenue for your business.

The purpose of a coach is to help others explore their desires, deepest thoughts, emotions and needs and to make changes in their lives that will bring personal and/or business success.

A coach should also provide support to clients, be able to listen and respond effectively, ask for assistance when necessary, share his or her thoughts in a rational and effective manner and also to maintain your own self-esteem while coaching others.

""Running a Coaching Business: An Introductory Guide to Running Your First Coaching Program" will take you through the basic steps of realizing a dream of becoming a coach and helping others through your expertise.

So You Want to Be a Coach?

If you're thinking about becoming a coach, you should know that a variety of coaching professions have greatly increased in popularity over the past decade. This has been largely because the emergence of successful online businesses and the need and desire of others to learn how to be an online success.

Anyone with the skills and a desire to coach can train others to succeed in a chosen profession or simply enjoy a better lifestyle. Coaching involves training others to do what they desire to do, but lack the knowledge or skills to put it into action.

You should also know that there are many types of online coaching. The ones we'll be concentrating on in this guide are:

- **Online Marketing Coach** - Coaches for online marketers should already be successful online marketers. Online marketing is an extremely popular way to make money and run your own business today and becoming an online marketing coach can be a lucrative way to make money teaching others.

- **Life Coach** - Techniques involved with becoming a life coach involve skills that may have mainly been learned in sociology, career counseling and psychology. Life coaches provide guidance and some types of guidance may require a degree in many states.

- **Business Coach** - This type of coaching involves support and advice to a business group so that the effectiveness of the business is increased. A business coach may specialize in teaching executives, overall business coaching or coaching for leadership.

All of the above coaching businesses can be developed online and can become a great base for creating webinars, products and other ways to bring in a passive income.

Bringing Out Your Coaching Skills

Anyone can be a coach who has the desire and skills to help others achieve success in their personal lives or businesses. Coaching is different from managing, mentoring, training and counseling. Here are the differences between the types of techniques:

- **Manager** - Sees that employees know how to perform a certain job.

- **Mentor** - Teaching how other successful people operate.

- **Trainer** - Instructing others to build skills in a certain area.

- **Counselor** - Helping others develop solutions for problems or issues.

Some of these techniques may cross over in the business of coaching, but mainly a coach helps others to identify skills that the person desires and wants to cultivate and helping others live up to their potential.

A great coach has a wide variety of communication skills, including the art of listening to the person, clarifying objectives and helping others find their own solutions and paths that will achieve their goals.

Why Become a Coach?

There are so many advantages to becoming an online coach - either as a part of your current online business-marketing plan or to fulfill a desire to help others become successful.

Observing a client make the changes necessary to reach the next level of personal or business success is a privilege that most of us don't get to see. When your clients begin to return in the future and thank you for all you've done for them, you'll only then begin to see the impact you've had on lives and businesses.

You may be thinking about becoming a coach because of one or many of the following reasons:

- **Reaching others on a global basis**. Thanks to the Internet, you can now contact others all over the world in a matter of nanoseconds. The advantage to your established online business could be an enormous opportunity for you to expand and bring in revenue from another source.

- **Online coaching is convenient**. In this busy world, convenience and saving time is a major consideration to people when enlisting a new service. Busy business owners and others don't have time to arrange sessions during the day and rely on meetings at night or at their convenience. Computers have made the difference so that a person can be coached at any time.

- **Helps you reach your own business goals**. Taking a motivational stance with others can easily help you work through your own issues and get results that you've longed for. It's a type of "reverse coaching" that by helping others, you're actually helping yourself.

- **Helps you reach personal goals**. Whether you're an online coach or a meetin-person type coach, you're bound to discover new things about yourself during the process of helping others. You may be shy to meeting and opening up to others, but when you coach online, the Internet provides the medium so that you can begin to feel more comfortable.

Behind every great person, there's likely a coach or mentor who has helped him or her achieve that level of greatness. Every successful business had dreamers and deep thinkers that worked hard and overcame obstacles to reach the pinnacle that very few have experienced.

There aren't too many professions other than coaching that can truly claim they've have a part in helping to create and encourage someone to reach their true potentials. That, alone, is a great reason for choosing coaching as a profession.

Credentials Needed for Online Coaching

To become a successful online marketing, life or business coach, you should first research and find which coach training program is appropriate for you. Many coaching programs offer a way for you to list yourself as a "coach-in-training" so that you can get started as soon as you feel comfortable.

Below is a list of ways you can learn to become an online coach in the three ways listed in this guide:

- **Online Marketing Coach** - Becoming a successful online marketing coach simply requires that you have already earned a high degree of success in Internet marketing. There's a huge demand for online marketing coaches who have become entrepreneurs and are ready to teach others their strategies.

- **Online Life Coach** - Life coaches who pursue online businesses should have some learning credentials such as the ICF (International Coach Federation) accredited training program. You may be able to list yourself as a coach-intraining while you're learning to help you get exposure. To get some one-on- one practice, you can offer free or discounted sessions.

- **Online Business Coach** - As so many large corporations and other types of businesses take their training and other programs online, becoming an online business coach makes good sense. Most businesses ask for credentials and the ICF has fully-accredited programs for various levels. If you've had excellent experience in coaching businesses successfully, you can offer that for credentials.

The appropriate credentials are very important in presenting yourself as an online coach, but if you have already built a name in your chosen field, you can proceed by following the instructions offered in the remainder of this guide, "Running a Coaching Business: An Introductory Guide to Running Your First Coaching Program."

Main Learning Points of Section One

It takes some work on yourself and a lot of research before you should set up an online office for your coaching business. You may already have vast experience in the business world, but when you coach others you'll need to first pin down the type of coach you want to be and the skills you need.

"Section One: So You Want to Be a Coach?" guides you in the process of choosing the type of coaching you want to concentrate on and what you need to set up your own coaching business.

• Three popular types of coaches are marketing, life or business coach.

• Online coaching is different from mentoring, training, managing and counseling.

• Certain skills, experience and credentials may be needed to set yourself up as a successful online coach no matter which type of coaching you choose.

- Things to think about before choosing to coach. There are many advantages to you, personally and in your own online business.

- You should ascertain which coaching niche you'd like to work towards.

Building Your Coaching Program

Before you begin your coaching program, you'll want to have a plan in place that will help you stay on track when you're up and running. A good business person always has a blueprint for his or her business that will help provide direction - just like architectural drawings for building a house.

This section of "So You Want to Be a Coach?" will provide direction you can use to develop your own coaching program. It's as easy as "following the yellow brick road" to the payoff of having built a lucrative and thriving coaching business.

Choose Your Coaching Niche

This first step may seem obvious, but after you choose a type of coaching, you may need to narrow it down to actually target the audience you're looking for. If you make the topic too wide, you risk the chance of losing business because of lack of understanding.

For example, if you want to coach beginner Internet marketers, be sure you convey that understanding in your advertising, coaching website and blog posts. Here are five key tasks for developing your own coaching program:

1. **Choose a coaching preference**. Future coaches who have a background in psychology, counseling and perhaps are already accredited by the ICF may want to honor their skills by becoming a life coach.

Narrowing down the topic may mean that you choose to specialize in coaching people in their career choices, relationships or lifestyles. After you choose a coaching preference, you're ready to do some research.

2. Research how others are coaching in your chosen topic. You can learn a lot from how a coaching business should be run by checking out other coaches in your niche.

What techniques are other coaches using to attract clients? What advertising methods are they using and what types of websites have they set up?

3. Time to brainstorm. At some point in your strategic planning and choosing a niche, you've got to take some time to brainstorm what you already know about the niche.

If you're already successful in the niche you're going to be coaching others in, you've got a head start. You likely already have websites and content set up that you can use.

Beginning coaches may need to take some online courses and take the time to become accredited in a chosen niche. You may want to consult with others to get even more out of the brainstorming sessions.

4. Organize your knowledge into teachable modules. After you've chosen your coaching niche, it's time to organize the material into teachable sections that will flow well and give you an idea about where you need to "fill in the blanks."

You may want to turn the modules into eBooks, newsletters and e-courses to help generate revenue right away. Also, look into ways you can automate your coaching practice so that less time is spent on technical details.

5. Decide how you're going to deliver your coaching expertise. Thanks to the Internet, there are many methods from which you can choose to get the word out about your coaching business.

Part of your marketing strategy should be a combination of delivery methods that can reach a wider audience. You can easily provide videos, content, live calls, webinars and more that will attract traffic to your sites and develop and audience - and clients for your coaching practice.

Take the necessary time to choose a coaching niche and develop a program that your audience will want to pay money for. A successful online coaching business should bring you personal fulfillment and a great branch of revenue for your online business pursuits.

Remember, it doesn't matter how great you are at coaching others in a chosen niche unless you're prepared with a plan of action that can lead you successfully through roadblocks and issues that you're bound to face.

The next section, "Best Practices for Running a Coaching Program" will take you to the next step of seffing up a successful online coaching program by avoiding certain practices and making sure you have other essential practices firmly in place.

Main Learning Points of Section Two

Every successful business begins with a good plan of action. You may want to immediately jump into the practice of coaching others, but before you do, you need to thoroughly think through some of the main issues of seWng up and running an online coaching business.

In "Section Two: Building Your Program," the following techniques were discussed that should help you build a successful coaching program:

• Use the skills you already have to choose a coaching niche.

• Narrow down the niche if the subject is too wide. For example, you may want to become a life coach, but narrow it even further by choosing to become a life coach for women.

• Brainstorming by yourself or with others is a great way to develop your coaching program.

• Decide how you're going to deliver your coaching advice - videos and webinars are just a couple of methods to consider.

• Spend some time researching how other successful coaches have set up their coaching programs.

• A plan of action is necessary before you begin the coaching process. Don't neglect the details as you set up your program and begin to formulate your marketing and selling techniques.

Best Practices for Running an Online Coaching Program

The coaching process should help your clients achieve success and live up to their full potential as individuals or part of a team. SeWng up an ethical and lucrative coaching practice means that you must know what to make an integral part of your practice - and what to avoid.

It's important that you select the right pricing options for your clients, whether you're coaching one-on-one or in groups, such as for a corporation. This is an important part of seWng up your coaching business because it can determine how you attract clients and help you determine what your bottom line is for your coaching services.

Pricing Options for Your Coaching Practice

Before you make a decision about pricing, you need to determine how you're going to offer your services. For example, you can request payment by individual sessions, payment by month or a six month package deal.

When your clients are encouraged to purchase coaching packages, they'll be more likely to stick to the commitment. Also, your income is more stable and you can better predict future revenue by staggering appointments appropriately.

Giving your clients a discount for purchasing a monthly or months-long package deal may also be appealing to them. But, some clients will want to pay by the session - at least until they get to know you better.

Common coaching fees for the U.S. can run from $100 for an individual session, $400 for a month and $2400 for a six-month package. Of course, you can vary your prices, depending on how much experience and credentials you have.

Many new coaches or those who are working on accreditation offer discounts early on so they can get the practice they need while learning. It's a win-win for the client and for the coach to be earning money and learning at the same time.

If you're going to offer a coaching package, there are several things you'll want to consider:

1. How many sessions will your clients receive and how long will the sessions last? Again, look at how other coaches in your niche are formulating their sessions. Think of ways you can offer them even more.

2. Are you going to offer additional "perks" and client support in your package deals? Value add-ons such as written material or eBooks, email access if they have questions, periodic assessments and phone calls may all be desirable in a client coaching package.

3. Pricing your package also depends on your target audience and the nature of your niche, plus your background, credentials and experience. You can always offer discounted prices if you're in the process of receiving credentials or you lack a lot of on-the-job experience.

4. Consider having more than one coaching package that you offer for different prices. When you offer low, medium and higher-priced packages, you ensure serving a wider range of clients. Some clients are willing to pay ahead for future services if the package offers value and the price is right.

5. Research the pricing for the coaching niche you've chosen to select more accurate pricing. For example, a life coach

may receive a lesser price point than a coach who teaches high level business executives.

The good news is that you can always change the pricing if you find that it isn't working for you.

Practices You Should Incorporate in Your Online Coaching Business

The rewards for enlightening and helping people on their paths to success and personal fulfillment can be many, both personally and financially. With online coaching, technology is available for you to help clients all over the world and to use your coaching business to build your list and drive traffic to your other online business pursuits.

Here are some sure-fire strategies that other successful online coaches have developed and that you should consider incorporating in your own coaching practice:

• Before you begin, be sure you have the necessary skills and qualifications. Prospective clients will shy away immediately if they perceive that you lack the necessary experience and skills to successfully help them rise to their potential in the coaching niche you've chosen.

• Listen and ask questions that will help you understand the client's circumstances and state of mind. Get to know your client by gently leading him or her to answer pertinent questions.

• Discover the goals, both hidden and spoken, of the client. Whether you're coaching business executives or a newly married couple, you'll have to lead them in the right goal-seffing directions.

• Use tools and proven techniques in your counseling session. "Homework" assignments may be a good technique to help a person sort out their thoughts and feelings in the privacy of his home.

Stress to your client that he should make a commitment to act on change and practice the changes so that it becomes a permanent path of facilitating positive outcomes.

• Work within the client's competence level. If you're talking or providing materials that are over his head he'll lose interest quickly and may quit the sessions out of frustration.

Always be non-judgmental and positive with clients. Don't be afraid to ask for feedback at the close of a session. You need to know what the client learned to assess whether or not you're on the right track.

26

What to Avoid When Running an Online Coaching Practice

Besides the definite practices that you'll do well to incorporate into your online coaching business there are certain situations you should avoid. You can avoid misunderstandings and miscommunication with your client by avoiding the following:

• Avoid becoming subjective when it comes to your client. If your client has issues with someone or something in his life or business, objectivity is key in being able to evaluate and lead your client to make his own, healthy decisions.

• Avoid leAVIng your clients develop a dependency on your coaching. Encourage them to develop independent thinking and to work out (with your help) what it will take to achieve their goals.

•Never send your clients to a webpage, book or other online material without checking it out first. There are many scams in cyberspace and misinformation. Be sure that the sites you choose to help your clients are legitimate.

•If you don't know the answer to a question or know how to point your client in the right direction, don't be afraid to tell him. You can be helpful by offering to help him find the answers to the problem and get back to him later or point to other information that may help.

You can become an excellent life, business or online marketing coach with some hard work and focus on doing everything possible to help your clients succeed. Besides ethics, it takes commitment, determination and patience to build your coaching practice into one that will be both fulfilling and profitable.

The next section, "Marketing & Selling," deals with the marketing, advertising and selling part of your online coaching business. The approaches will vary somewhat because of the niche you choose, but the basics that you need to begin will get you started.

Main Learning Points of Section Three

Running an online coaching business parallels running a brick and mortar business in many ways. You have to know how to price your coaching services just as you would have to price merchandise and you need to know how to incorporate certain practices and avoid others.

Below is the "short" version of what was offered in Section Three: Best Practices for Running an Online Coaching Program:

- Price your coaching services so that you attract the target audience of your niche. Offering several types of coaching packages could be good for business and can help you plan ahead.

- Incorporate practices in your online coaching business that reflect the ethics and experience you have for your niche.

- Listen carefully to your clients so that you can use your expertise to put them on the path to success.

- Worth within your client's competence level. Don't offer advice or information that's over his head or bore him by offering coaching techniques that he may already be familiar with.

- Strive to get a commitment from your client about seriously working on the issues that can help him succeed.

- Some practices you should avoid in your online coaching practice include becoming subjective to your clients' problems, offering information without first looking at it and offering advice without having the knowledge or experience to know if it's right.

Marketing & Selling Your Online Coaching Program

Thanks to the incredible technology of the 21st Century, you now have virtually thousands of ways to market and sell your ideas and techniques in your online coaching business.

This section will offer a few methods that have proven best for most successful online entrepreneurs, including online coaches. You want to make a good first impression to your audience, so that means that your marketing and selling points and material need to be classy, concise and straightforward.

Some key issues that you need to remember when working out your marketing and selling strategies are:

- **It doesn't have to be perfect to begin**. After you release the plan to the World Wide Web, you'll soon be able to ascertain if the strategy is going to work - or not. Learn from the response and then tweak and update to make it better.

- **Build your list by releasing some of your well-thought out program free to prospective clients**. If a visitor

30

wants and needs coaching advice, he'll almost surely take you up on receiving some materials for free - and then following up with consultations if he likes what he sees.

• **Consider offering a free consultation**. It's a great way for prospective clients to get to know you and your level of expertise and for you to get to know what type of clients you're attracting with your marketing strategies.

When you're sure the client is a good fit, ask that he sign up for coaching services. If not, tell him why you don't think the relationship will work and help him find another coach.

•**If you already have an online business and are branching out into coaching, use your present list to gain clients or testimonials for your coaching site.**

You don't have to sell your list at this point. Simply tell them of your plans and tell them you'd appreciate referrals if they know of anyone in need of your new service.

•**Offer a discount to your first clients and ask them for testimonials.**

Discounts are always a great drawing factor for first time coaching clients. It gives them a chance to see how your expertise can help them achieve their dreams.

Those are just some basic tips for implementing your marketing and selling strategy. The next part of this section deals with the specifics of designing and selling your online coaching services.

Designing Your Marketing Strategy

A good online marketing strategy is one that's designed to drive traffic and acquire clients for your business. It makes sense to learn how other, successful, marketers are doing it and mimic them - but with your own spin. This strategy will save you money in the long run because you won't be spinning your wheels.

As you'll see when you research successful online coaching businesses, they likely have the following strategies in place that made their businesses successful:

•**Make your main website the hub of your business strategies.** Most prospective clients will do their beginning research by visiting your website.

Make sure it's easily navigated and explains how you do business and how you can help them with their coaching needs.

Your website needs to contain personal information such as your background and a personal story about what led you into

32

coaching. Testimonials are a must, so be sure to elicit those from your first group of clients.

Make the content conversational. Don't scare them off or bore them with too much information, but be clear about what you're offering and what advantages there will be for the client.

- **Bundle your services**. Bundling and packaging is a way for your potential clients to see that he's going great value for his money. Offering discounts or a free first consultation is also a way to give them value when choosing your services.

You can learn a lot by seeing how other coaching entrepreneurs are packaging their services - but be sure to make yours different and offer even more value for the money spent.

- **Give your future clients value.** If you offer free materials as a bonus when signing up for your mailing list, be sure it contains awesome information that they can really use.

Think about what would appeal to your niche clients and write or present the content accordingly.

- **Use the up sell strategy**. A great campaign might include an up sell offer that either gives your client a discount for your services or provides them with some special information that they miss out on if they don't sign up. Make it clearly worth their while to consider.

33

Up selling has been an effective marketing strategy for many online entrepreneurs. There's a ton of information online about how to develop this unique strategy into one that will work well for you.

It's important to keep the lines of communication open with both clients and prospective clients. Don't bombard them with emails and sales pitches, but offer some valuable information when you do make contact with them.

When you offer value for a client's time and money, you're ensuring a lasting relationship and future success for you and the client.

Selling Your Coaching Services

Making money from your online coaching business means that you have to ask prospective clients for the business. You don't have to use overly-ambitious sales methods, but simply be yourself.

The sale begins when you creatively tell clients what you can help them with and ask them if they might be interested in your services. Pay attention to what their needs might be and what the outcome can be if they choose you for their coach.

You may get some who say, "No," but those who say "Yes" can get you started in a lucrative online coaching business that can be satisfying and fulfilling for you and the clients.

There are many ways that you can close a sale online:

• **Email Campaigns** - The heart of any online marketer's business, good email campaigns can set your business up for ultimate success. If you're already successful in an online business, you likely succeeded in part because of a great email campaign.

• **Advertising** - Spend the dollars of your advertising budget wisely by researching what methods other successful online coaches are using to drive traffic and attract clients. Make your ad stand by being clear in your statements and eye-catching in its design.

• **Social Media** - Sites such as Facebook, LinkedIn, Google+ and more are excellent ways to brand your coaching business and build relationships with clients and future clients.

• **Webinars and Videos** - You can really set yourself up as an expert by showing off your expertise by hosting a webinar or creating a video that introduces your coaching services. Be sure to offer great value in either one. Time is valuable these days and no one wants to waste time and effort by viewing or participating in something where they don't learn anything.

Investing some real time and effort in your sales methods can reap huge benefits -- and revenue. The bottom line is that when people perceive that they're getting lots of value for their time and money, they're likely to sign the contract with that person over any other.

Take the time to develop your marketing and selling strategies to reap the most benefits.

Main Learning Points of Section Four

Here are some highlights of what you learned in Section Four:

- Don't wait until you have a perfect marketing and selling strategy. The feedback you'll receive will tell you if you're on the right path.

- The design and content of your coaching website should be the hub of your marketing and selling strategy.

- Be sure to include personal information and testimonials in your website.

- Bundle information and coaching offers to include discounts, free bonus reports and other attractive offerings.

36

- Always give your prospective clients and present clients value in any material you offer.

- Use the up sell strategy to get your clients to want more of what you have to offer.

- Use email campaigns, social media, advertising, webinars and videos to get the word out about your coaching business and to help make the sale.

CONCLUSION

Although "Running a Coaching Business: An Introductory Guide to Running Your First Coaching Program" may not address everything you ever wanted to know about online coaching, it's a great way to learn about the basics if you want to develop a successful online coaching program.

It provides some helpful hints in deciding if you're ready for the online coaching experience. Coaching can be extremely rewarding, both personally and financially, but it will take time and effort.

You also learned about what steps you need to take to build your online coaching business the right way by choosing your coaching niche according to your own desires, experience and expertise and how to narrow it down and organize your knowledge into teachable modules.

Pricing your services can be a daunting task, but this guide will show you the strategies you need to take in pricing according to your experience and credentials.

Using the appropriate teaching techniques and tools in your online coaching program is essential if you want to build the reputation of delivering what you promised.

There are certain practices that you should definitely make a part of your business and those that you should avoid. These practices may apply to others online business areas than coaching. Learning how to formulate your coaching program practices can set you up for success or failure.

If you don't know how to market and sell your coaching services, you won't be able to take your business to a profitable and satisfying level. This guide offered the basics about marketing and selling techniques.

You learned that you don't have to wait until the marketing program is perfect before you begin your practice, but can learn how to change and tweak it when you begin to receive feedback.

Begin by designing your market strategy with a great design and content for your website. Then, you can branch out into other areas to drive traffic and ensure sales.

Social media, webinars, videos and other methods can give you the advantages you need to compete with other online coaching services. This guide provided a basic list of ways you can be sure you're giving your clients value each time they visit your site or view your advertisements.

Staying competitive in the online coaching business means that you must continuously develop your skills and learn more about the niche you chose for your business.

Hopefully, this guide, "Running a Coaching Business: An Introductory Guide to Running Your First Coaching Program" has answered your basic questions about beginning or branching out into life coaching, business or coaching Internet marketers.

Every step you take to make sure you're starting out your coaching pursuits on the right foot will ensure your success and help you ensure the quality of the services you offer your clients.

Printed by Libri Plureos GmbH in Hamburg, Germany